Don't Ask Dumb Questions!

SIDNEY S. PRASAD

DEDICATION

This book is dedicated to Shree Gurudev Datta.

CONTENTS

ACKNOWLEDGMENTS

It's common for a lot of educators and trainers to look forward to and invite questions from their pupils. In fact they will reinforce that no question is dumb unless it's not asked. But on the contrary we have all heard the most bizarre, silliest questions ever asked. We sometimes debate if the person is just plain outright stupid or just really ignorant.

I have always pondered if my superiors regret opening the channels of discussion and inviting those curious imbeciles to contribute their irrelevant questions. So I decided to poke some fun at those yahoos and create a book that stressed Don't Ask Dumb Questions!

1 DUMBEST QUESTIONS

Do people walk in Rome?

Do cemetery workers only work graveyard shifts?

Do you need to make an appointment to see a psychic?

Do gullible people eat suckers?

Do people in Bangkok have sore dicks?

Do racists drive professionally for a living?

Do people who live in caves always give in?

Do tow truck drivers have foot fetishes?

Do people only eat chicken in Kentucky?

Do boxers live in the Rocky Mountains?

Are people starving in Hungary?

Are people in a hurry in Russia?

Are there sex addicts in the Virgin Islands?

Are people dying to get to the graveyard?

Are ties made in Thailand?

Are there French hookers in Lahore?

Are people spiritual in Seoul?

Are werewolves lost?

Are Vampires prime A.I.D.S. candidates?

Are you suppose to move away if there is a car coming at you that say's "Dodge" on the front?

Is there a Hilton in Paris?

Is salad technically naked without dressing?

Is spell-check for witches?

Is the Easter Bunny from Easter Island?

Is a shoehorn loud?

Is the boardroom a storage for wood?

If a car that contained four passengers drove off a cliff and landed in the sea, is that considered carpooling?

Is Black Friday an ethnic holiday?

Is a Happy Meal the same concept as an antidepressant pill?

Is capital punishment when your parents cut your allowance off?

DON'T ASK DUMB QUESTIONS!

Is a bulldozer a sleeping mammal?

Is the Dead Sea a flat piano note?

Does it make sense to put locks on the doors of doughnut shops that are open 24/7?

Does it make sense for your doctor to leave the room while you undress before a breast examination?

Does Michael come from Jordan?

Does Lysol get rid of lice?

Does Home Depot sell houses?

Does Satan cook in Hell's Kitchen?

Does it make sense to call a vegetarian a meathead?

Does the Cable Guy eat TV dinners?

Does the Royal Family dine at Burger King and Dairy Queen?

Does smoked salmon require rolling paper?

Can a self-employed person file sexual harassment charges against themself?

Can a store issue a rain check on a sunny day?

Can you feed animal crackers to a vegetarian?

Can you eat a TV dinner if you don't have cable?

Can you take a nap in a restroom?

Can you eat a hot dog on a cold day?

Can a gay person be miserable?

Can you have a dead person in your living room?

Can morbidly obese people go skinny dipping?

Can dumb people eat Smarties?

Can an exterminator get rid of a bookworm?

Can you buy fresh meat in New Delhi?

If someone has a bottle of glue inside a mental hospital, is that called Crazy Glue?

If a publisher can't sell books, do they have to file for Chapter 11 Bankruptcy?

If you have a hand transplant is that considered second-hand?

If one were to practice witchcraft in the desert, does that make them a sandwich?

If one were to drop club soda on their shirt, how would they remove the stain?

DON'T ASK DUMB QUESTIONS!

Do you need a crane to shoplift?

Do people cry in Argentina?

Do poles come from Poland?

Do birds eat their lunch on Sesame Street?

Why do stand-up comedians bring chairs to the stage?

Why aren't cheapskates scared of falling on the ice?

Why don't game shows invite employment benefits recipients and people on welfare to their show? Because they can totally use the money!

Why can't babies sleep like adults?

Why do people keep stealing Webster's dictionary?

Why do unemployed Quarterbacks complain that they are penniless?

Why do parents put wagon wheels in their children's lunch?

Did an exterminator kill The Beatles?

How many name tags do you give to someone with multiple personalities?

How do you give crap to someone in sign language?

Is a crash course dangerous?

Are hoes tools for promiscuous gardeners?

Are you supposed to donate seeds to a grassroots charity?

Are there carpets in the animal shelter?

Are cannibals a non-perishable food item?

Are there chef schools in the Cook Islands?

Are people cold in Chile?

Are there a lot of clubs in Monaco?

Are people contagious in Germany?

Are Greyhounds supposed to be grey?

Are people that live on manors well behaved?

Do lumberjacks have their meetings in boardrooms?

Do you have to be dead to wear your heart on your sleeve?

Do babysitters sit on babies?

Do highways refer to instructional methods while impaired under the influence of illegal drugs?

Do rappers work at gift shops?

DON'T ASK DUMB QUESTIONS!

Do people get their ass kicked on Boxing Day?

Do Eskimos have their assets frozen?

Do people jump on leap year?

Do cats believe in reincarnation since they have nine lives?

Do people graffiti their TV room walls in Denmark?

Do people kiss with their tongues touching in France?

Do people wear capes in Cape Town?

Do people drive Hyundai's in Santa Fe?

Do people chew tobacco in Copenhagen?

Do people eat sandwiches on the subway?

What is the admission at the movies for someone with multiple personalities?

Why the heck are there cup-holders in cars if drinking and driving is illegal?

Is solar power spiritual energy?

Is the Milky Way an address for a dairy farm?

Is break dancing destructive behavior?

Is Starbucks space money for astronauts?

Is having dinner with a handicap person sort of like a blind date?

Is the Big Apple really fruity?

Is Old Dutch a geriatric German person?

Is the AA Group a place for people that stutter?

Is Harry Potter a horticulturist that needs to shave badly?

Is a window cleaner the same concept as a computer technician?

Where is China made?

Is a charley horse the name of an animal that you bet on at the track?

2 STUPID QUESTIONS

Do you have to be a farmer in order to have a cow?

Do cannibals put their heads together?

Do serial killers ruin people's breakfast?

Do midgets eat shortcake?

Do carpenters shop at Wall Street?

Do you have to be open-minded in order to get brain surgery?

Do reindeers use umbrellas?

Do skyscrapers require Band-Aids?

Do stalkers work at warehouses?

Do pots grow in pantries?

Do cannibals give good head?

Do Jocks wash their clothes at the bleachers?

Can a dyslexic person eat alphabet soup?

Can an ugly guy have a hotmail account?

Can a priest be called father if he doesn't have any kids?

Can a Caucasian woman get blackmailed?

Can females have cockfights?

Can you return sour dough?

Can you buy walls on Wall Street?

Does Iron Man have wrinkled clothes?

Does Joan Rivers empty into the sea?

Does eating light involve swallowing light bulbs?

Does the Headless Horseman have a Facebook page?

Does Church's Chicken belong to the clergy?

Does kidnap mean when a child goes to sleep?

Does a kingdom refer to stupid royalty?

Does the first class section of the airplane come with a teacher?

Is a con artist a criminal that likes to paint?

Is Dancing With The Stars a show about astronomy?

Is a pen friend someone that works for Staples?

DON'T ASK DUMB QUESTIONS!

Is poker another word for sex?

Is a coward a designated area in the animal hospital for large mammals?

Is a backhoe a hooker in the alley?

Are the Oscars, awards for grouchy people?

Is a taxi someone the I.R.S. is looking for?

Is a crack addict someone that enjoys staring at people's asses?

Is George Burns a pyromaniac?

Are cell phones for prisoners?

Are horny people instrumental?

Are musician's assistants called Band-Aids?

Are pioneers close to getting their desserts?

Are contests examinations for criminals?

Are potheads dubious?

Are golfers aloud to drink coffee during tee time?

Are crooked optometrists icons?

Is a diehard someone who died with an erection?

Is a groundhog a fat ass sun tanner?

Is Tiger Woods an African forest?

Is a cocktail the end of a penus?

Are cartoons and a car stereo the same concept?

Is an optometrist an eyewitness?

Is a hamstring an edible rope?

Is horticulture a religion about sluts?

Is a furnace the bum of a plant?

Is a dogma the mother of a mutt?

If artists didn't exist how would we see the big picture?

If your doorbell malfunctions is it considered a dumbbell?

If you lost a bottle is that a jargon?

If you repeatedly type stereo is that considered stereotyping?

If two locksmiths got into a quarrel are they considered warlocks?

If you ride a horse at night do you need a satellite?

Is a couch potato organic furniture?

DON'T ASK DUMB QUESTIONS!

Is Austin Powers an electric company in Texas?

Is a doggy bag a puppy's luggage?

Is a landmark agriculture graffiti?

Is a landlord a religious figure?

Is mayhem a spring pig?

Is a console the spirit of a con artist?

Is a broadcast a female bandage?

Is a whiner an alcoholic?

Is a cinema the mother of an evil sinner?

Was the Great Depression a shortage of happy pills?

Was Desert Storm a machine malfunction at Dairy Queen?

Do alcoholics wear tank tops?

Can jailbirds fly?

Why don't people get wet when they play pool?

Did a cannibal invent Facebook?

Can you get in shit for taking a shit on a craps table?

Does a guy's manhood protect his head from extreme weather conditions?

Can an invoice shut up?

Is protein someone who supports teenagers?

Is Rummage the Post Prohibition era?

Is a pumpkin Barbie's boyfriend on steroids?

Is Santa Claus a legal Christmas loophole?

Is handicap an accessible hat?

Is a lama a singing mother?

Is there a time limit to watch 60 Minutes?

Is a massacre a large piece of land?

Do parasites have double vision?

Is a petticoat an animal sweater?

3 CORKIEST QUESTIONS

Is Coffee-Mate a friendly beverage companion?

Is a chili dog a South American mammal?

Does irony refer to someone with a metal leg?

Can you buy a caffeine free T-shirt?

Is gravy considered a morbid term?

Do actors who reenact crime scenes ever get arrested for resembling the wanted criminals they were portraying?

Is Congress the opposite of progress?

Does a Police Officer tell a Mute they have the right to remain silent?

If a teacher tells you to pay attention, are they hinting for a bribe?

Do untruthful people lie in bed?

Do mass murderers only kill fat people?

Are refried beans leftovers?

What was the cause of death of the Dead Sea?

Can homeless people eat cottage cheese?

How does the garbage man decipher if your trash can is garbage?

Do drug addicts drive on highways?

Is a humanitarian the opposite of a cannibal?

If someone claims that they are speechless, then technically they made a statement right?

Do actors eat TV dinners?

How come nobody invented B size batteries?

Can a vegetarian use duck tape?

Are flying saucers used for serving fast food?

Is goodwill when you receive a large inheritance?

Why are apartments attached to each other?

Should badminton players be reported to the Animal Rights Commission for hitting all those birdies?

What is the definition of definition?

If you are breathing and alive then how do you get a life?

Does the SWAT team kill mosquitoes?

DON'T ASK DUMB QUESTIONS!

Can you skip a jump rope test?

Can a paraplegic take a stand?

What is the opposite of falling in love?

Is Iran a past tense race?

Is a soap opera clean music?

Are doughnuts a negative stereotype referring to crazy fat people?

Rather than having chains on their pens, why don't bankers lock their pens in the vault?

Do produce managers drive lemons?

Is it illegal to graffiti a wall using invisible ink?

Are manically depressed people allowed at Happy hour?

Do cameras have photographic memories?

If a houseboat sank underwater would the sink sink as well?

Do panhandlers work in cookware stores?

Who does a policeman call when he gets robbed?

Is it offensive to ask a vegan if they got milk?

Is pot roast cooked marijuana?

Is Shakespeare an epileptic weapon?

Is it politically correct to call a first year female student a freshman?

Does stereotyping involve keying stories about music players?

Are pleasant males referred to as mankind?

Is a pop quiz a test about Pepsi?

Do you have to be really flexible to be head over heels for someone?

Is it possible to trip over a cordless phone?

What was the best thing prior to sliced bread?

If love is blind then does hate have 20/20 vision?

Why pay money to go to the top of a building and then pay more money to use a telescope to look down?

Wouldn't it make sense for a Vampire to open a blood donor clinic?

Do cows have calf muscles?

Do hogs eat like pigs?

Is baking a piece of cake?

Is the use of a handgun considered cheating during an arm wrestle?

Can a cop book a librarian?

Are waiters' patient?

Are patients' patient?

Are drug addicts dopey?

Are sugar daddies diabetic?

Are lactose intolerance astronauts allowed in the Milky Way?

Is a nightmare a sleep walking horse?

Is a mistletoe the kiss of death?

Do people jump around at IHOP?

Does bootleg refer to the geographic shape of Italy?

Is a health nut someone who is on a crazy diet?

Do people get snappy if they don't get their finger food right away?

Does anybody know Victoria's Secret?

Can you get a lot of vitamin C living in Orange County?

Do doormen enjoy shutting people out?

Are bouncers on the rebound?

Do adulterers cheat on matrimonial tests?

Are operators phony?

Are cliff notes key points about a ridge?

If a carpenter doesn't charge you for a roof is it on the house then?

Is a cowboy a male calf?

Is Santa Barbara located in the North Pole?

Is fruit punch a boxer from Orange County?

Are questions questionable?

Can a comedian get hurt by a bad punch line?

Is a matchmaker someone that makes toys for pyromaniacs?

Do cradle robbers enjoy stealing baby furniture?

How come there are no man fingers okra?

DON'T ASK DUMB QUESTIONS!

Can a potty be defined as a hot beverage containing marijuana?

Are dandelions well dressed mammals?

Can you buy walnuts at Home Depot?

Is a bandage the music era?

Is the boardwalk for people who have nothing to do?

Is a chestnut a crazy boob doctor?

Can you wear a phone booth?

Do deadbeats walk to a different tune?

Can you claim flood damage if your home has a sunken living room?

Does everyone have their work piled up on swamp land?

Can you return a free sample?

Do you need oil to grease a bouncer?

Are golden rules valuable?

What is the opposite of a dead-end?

Would you agree that degenerate gambling country bumpkins shouldn't bet the farm?

Do dump truck drivers stop for frequent shit-breaks?

Do perverted school presidents concentrate on pleasing the student body?

Do crowded kitchens have too many chefs in the kitchen?

Is feedback recycled food?

If people claim to call bullshit then does bullshit have a phone number?

4 CHEESIEST QUESTIONS

Can a rude criminal get a pardon?

What type of vehicle does a slave driver drive?

Is adultery a mature plant?

Do Mockingbirds imitate other birds?

Is Peter Pan the name of a cookware store?

Does it hurt to have a sidekick?

Do electricians complain about feeling wired?

Can a vegetarian catch the chicken pox?

Does a watchman work at Rolex?

Is Hamburger Helper a fast food employee?

What time does 7-11 close?

Is an autobiography the history of a vehicle?

Are bankrupt bakers short on doe?

Do holy men and saints live in the city of Angels?

Can you get ill if somebody sicks their dog on you?

Can fortune tellers predict bankruptcy?

Are there jailbirds at the zoo?

Are there busboys on Greyhounds?

Do firemen terminate employees?

Can you sleep in a knapsack?

Do prophets earn a lot of money?

Does Mr. Claus drive a Santa Fe?

Is there marine life in Wales?

Is a bag lady's father called Bagdad?

If a group cannibals ate a couple of Olympians in the morning, would that be considered breakfast of champions?

Do yellow-bellies need to work on their tan?

What type of boats do wholesalers take to the sea?

Is a female cover charge for a male?

Do craps dealers supply toilet paper?

Is a Shih Tzu a crappy lawyer?

Do airplane pilots enjoy getting high?

DON'T ASK DUMB QUESTIONS!

Do window cleaners work at Microsoft?

Do professional boxers work in warehouses?

Can you buy cars on Saturn?

Do gay bars have Happy hour all day?

Do celebrities complain about the draft from all their fans?

Is "The War On Terror" an attempt to ban horror movies?

Do boats have cruise control?

Is it incorrect to call a female priest Father?

Can a racist be color blind?

Do professional hit men earn a killing?

Did someone have to score a hole-in-one to win the Gulf War?

If the fire hall goes up in flames who puts out the fire?

Is a British Subject an English class?

Is it really slippery in Iceland?

Are sidewalks graded on the curb?

Are there a lot of roads in Rhode Island?

Do party poopers shit their pants at get-togethers?

Is a chairman a furniture salesman?

Are weed whackers used for "The War On Drugs?"

Does an Atheist have to swear on the Bible?

Do people eat chocolate bars on Mars?

Is hardwood a sexual term?

Do mountain climbers have rocky relationships?

Are there hotlines in Alaska?

Do you have to think about eating Wonder Bread?

Is Israel fake?

Does the mafia dine at God Father's Pizza?

Do engineers wear training bras during their probation period?

What do you call a female mailman?

Is a deadbeat a dying sound?

Is witchcraft evil artwork?

Do you have to bring a spoon to Super Bowl Sunday?

Can you end up in a hospital if you lose a game of Snakes and Ladders?

Is it rare to meet a single tailor since they enjoy tying the knot?

Do Marxists like graffiti?

Can females act cocky?

Is a basketball weaved out of straw?

If it's a penny for your thoughts, then are mind readers considered penny pinchers?

Are there June Bugs in May?

Are lubricants made in Greece?

Who do doctors call when they're sick?

Do headbangers need Aspirin?

Are cashmere sweaters made in India?

Does moonlighting involve flashing your bum in the light?

How come there are no traffic signs in Braille?

Do things get damaged in Rec Rooms?

Do Rednecks have rashes on their necks?

If girls get periods, then do guys get exclamation marks?

Can you sniff Pepsi?

Is a chain letter when someone mails you a necklace?

Are there rock stars in the alley?

Do florists make floors?

Is Johnny Cash a pay toilet?

Can a color blind person sing the blues?

Do you get a Bluetooth if you don't brush your teeth?

If somebody is two-faced, then do they have two Facebook accounts?

If a couple of seamen get lost at sea, then does the submarine have a low sperm count?

Are there animated dogs on Pluto?

Are people sick and loud in Illinois?

Do you have to be an electrician in order to power walk?

Do vegetarians eat crab apples?

Are alcoholics whiners?

Are brownie points bake sale frequent flyer miles?

If a waiter gets hungry after his shift, then who takes his order?

Is a carcass when one is affectionate towards their vehicle?

Do you need glasses to watch 20/20?

If cheese could talk, then what would it say when it got its picture taken?

5 NUTTIEST QUESTIONS

Don't you hate it when a jury finds you guilty for a crime that you didn't commit?

Don't you hate it when someone breaks into your house and racks up your phone bill?

Don't you hate it when your husband throws you a surprise birthday party one month after your birthday?

Don't you hate it when you are sleep walking and step on glass?

Don't you hate it when the person in the next toilet stall keeps asking you questions and breaks your concentration?

Don't you hate it when you get kicked out of sex education class for asking too many questions?

Don't you hate it when the phone wakes you up and it's the wrong number?

Don't you hate it when someone screams out the punch line before you finish telling your joke?

Don't you hate it when you have to give CPR to someone who just ate a chili dog?

Don't you hate it when you accidentally crash into a cop car?

DON'T ASK DUMB QUESTIONS!

Don't you hate it when someone licks the cream off your cookies?

Don't you hate it when your kids refuse to bail you out of jail?

Don't you hate it when your wife confesses to having a sex change prior to meeting you?

Don't you hate it when you buy someone a lottery ticket and they win the jackpot?

Don't you hate it when you get a tear in your panty hose and realize that you haven't shaved your legs in a month?

Don't you hate it when someone robs a bank and chooses you to be their hostage?

Don't you hate it when someone blows out your birthday candles for you?

Don't you hate it when you go trick-or-treating and someone gives you Ex-Lax?

Don't you hate it when your wife gets pregnant and forgets that you had a vasectomy?

Don't you hate it when your cooking instructor doesn't believe you that your dog ate your homework?

Don't you hate it when you flash someone and find out that they are blind?

Don't you hate it when your cross-dressing boyfriend wears your dress and looks better than you?

Don't you hate it when you go Dutch and the other person has a two for one coupon for their half?

Don't you hate it when someone asks a 7-11 employee what time they close?

Don't you hate it when you are attempting to call in sick at work and the phone lines are down?

Don't you hate it when the grocery store refuses to allow you to take the entire tray of free samples?

Don't you hate it when someone leaves their broken finger nail in the chip dip?

Don't you hate it when you are trying to rob a bank and the teller asks if you are going to your 20-year high school reunion?

Don't you hate it when your sister tells you a mama joke?

Don't you hate it when someone confuses you for a hooker and they end up being your father?

Don't you hate it when the waiter get's pissed off because you tipped him with Monopoly money?

Don't you hate it when you are panhandling and someone hand's you a counterfeit bill?

DON'T ASK DUMB QUESTIONS!

Don't you hate it when someone asks your twin sister how long she has known you for?

Don't you hate it when you are about to have sex and the phone rings and someone wants you to be their lifeline on a game show?

Don't you hate it when you are trying to cheat on a test and you can't read what the person next to you is writing?

Don't you hate it when your grandparents borrow your car and you find love stains on the backseat?

Don't you hate it when you mow over the lawn mower cord and get electrocuted?

Don't you hate it when your house guests are moaners?

Don't you hate it when someone steals your identity and earns more money using your Social Security number?

Don't you hate it when someone talks really close to you and has bad breath?

Don't you hate it when your employees call in sick on pay day?

Don't you hate it when you fall asleep in class and your teacher wakes you up?

Don't you hate it when your cross-dressing boyfriend bites into a doughnut and leaves a lipstick mark?

Don't you hate it when your neighbors peep through their window and catch you scratching your ass?

Don't you hate it when you are enjoying a meal at a restaurant and a mouse runs out of the kitchen?

Don't you hate it when you are hitchhiking and a cop picks you up?

Don't you hate it when someone regifts the exact same dollar store gift that you gave them last year?

Don't you hate it when a celebrity ball player autographs your baseball and misspells your name?

Don't you hate it when another vehicle hits your car and you get the blame?

Don't you hate it when someone copies your work and you get accused of plagiarism?

Don't you hate it when a waiter asks if you want your change back and assumes that you are willing to part with your nickel?

Don't you hate it when you purposely don't tip and you accidentally forget your purse in the restaurant?

Don't you hate it when your date finds takeout boxes in your garbage and realizes that you didn't cook dinner?

Don't you hate it when you are sun tanning and a bird poops on you?

DON'T ASK DUMB QUESTIONS!

Don't hate it when someone licks their fingers and then shakes your hand?

Don't you hate it when you get a paper cut on your ass from using cheap toilet paper?

Don't you hate it when you are doing a secret Santa at work and pick your own name?

Don't you hate it when you discover that your girlfriend has a husband that is your boss?

Don't you hate it when someone farts in an elevator and gives you a dirty look?

Don't you hate it when you bite into a cupcake and break your teeth because your wedding band slipped into the batter?

Don't you hate it when you ask someone a question and they ask you what you think?

Don't you hate it when you find out that your friend is a serial killer?

Don't you hate it when you drop the soap in the prison shower?

Don't you hate it when your babysitter decides to leave early and your kids' burn down your house?

Don't you hate it when you find out that your spouse is just using you for a Green Card?

Don't you hate it when you use insufficient postage to pay your utility bills and your electricity gets shut off?

Don't you hate it when you dial 911 and a mime answers the phone?

Don't you hate it when you show up to work and it's closed because it's a statutory holiday?

Don't you hate it when you get so drunk that you end up hitting on your boyfriend?

Don't you hate it when you heat up a TV dinner and forget to take the cardboard off?

Don't you hate it when you're getting freaky with your wife and accidentally call out your mother-in-law's name?

Don't you hate it when you are shining someone's shoes and they have dog poop on it?

Don't you hate it when you ask a stranger to take your picture and they run off with your camera?

Don't you hate it when the person at the drive-thru window tells you their life story?

Don't you hate it when you are waiting in line at the store and someone comes in and robs the place?

Don't you hate it when you are bobbing for apples and find a retainer?

DON'T ASK DUMB QUESTIONS!

Don't you hate it when the car ahead of you pays the tollbooth with pennies?

Don't you hate it when someone hacks into your email and sends your boss a resignation letter?

Don't you hate it when you accidentally cheer for the wrong team while sitting in the visitor section?

Don't you hate it when someone uses their cell phone in the airplane and causes the pilot to lose contact with the control tower?

Don't you hate it when you purchase something that requires assembly and the instructions are in a foreign language?

Don't you hate it when your neighbor's kid throws a baseball through your window and wakes you up?

Don't you hate it when your stockbroker loses your nest egg?

Don't you hate it when the person in front of you at the bank machine uses five different bank cards?

Don't you hate it when you fart and feel chocolate pudding in your underwear?

Don't you hate it when you accidentally blow your nose in a used maxi pad?

Don't you hate it when a cop won't accept a food stamp as a bribe?

Don't you hate it when people change their babies' poopy diapers in the food court?

Don't you hate it when someone borrows your flip flops and leaves toe jam in it?

Don't you hate it when your dog wipes his poopy tale on your pillow?

Don't you hate it when your date thinks you're cheap for tipping five percent?

Don't you hate it when your favorite pizza parlor gets shutdown for cremating bodies in their oven?

Don't you hate it when you forget to vote and your favorite candidate loses by one vote?

Don't you hate it when your friend borrows your jeans and leaves a skid mark for you?

Don't you hate it when someone sticks their eye on the other side of your door's peephole?

Don't you hate it when your tongue gets stuck to a frozen flagpole?

Don't you hate it when the movie theatre usher won't allow you to bring a video camera into the movie?

DON'T ASK DUMB QUESTIONS!

Don't you hate it when your waiter gives you a hassle for bringing in outside food?

Don't hate it when your waiter sits you next to the shitter and you can hear the gruesome echoes and flushes as you eat your food?

Don't you hate it when a health inspector shuts down the restaurant half way through your meal?

Don't you hate it when someone attempts to shake your hand at the urinal?

Don't you hate it when someone is eavesdropping on you while you're trying to take a crap?

Don't you hate it when you are hiding underneath your girlfriend's bed and you find out she is cheating on you?

Don't you hate it when your headlights die on you in the middle of a fog?

6 CORNIEST QUESTIONS

Don't you hate it when you run out of gas on the way to the bank machine?

Don't you hate it when a bird poops on your car right after you washed it?

Don't you hate it when you steal someone's wallet and there is only two dollars in it?

Don't you hate it when you are on hold for an hour and the cordless phone dies?

Don't you hate it when your girlfriend throws her used tampon in your garbage?

Don't you hate it when you accidentally drop your cell phone in the toilet?

Don't you hate it when your fly is undone and you are not wearing any underwear?

Don't you hate it when your date forgets their wallet?

Don't you hate it when a Ladybug pees on you?

Don't you hate it when someone brings a crying baby to the movie theater?

Don't you hate it when you get a crappy message inside a fortune cookie?

Don't you hate it when your blind date ends up being your ex-husband?

Don't you hate it when you find hair in your food?

Don't you hate it when you spill your drink and last call is over?

Don't you hate it when your private parts get caught in your zipper?

Don't you hate it when airport security questions you about the sex toys in your luggage?

Don't you hate it when you lock your keys in the get-a-way car?

Don't you hate it when your pencil breaks during a timed exam?

Don't you hate it when you are waiting in line for an hour and the tickets sell out?

Don't you hate it when you step on dog poop minutes before a job interview?

Don't you hate it when you miss the last bus and a cab ride home is eighty dollars?

Don't you hate it when your sunroof will not close and it starts raining?

Don't you hate it when someone steals your seat?

Don't you hate it when you have diarrhea and you run out of toilet paper?

Don't you hate it when the drive-thru forgets to give you ketchup?

Don't you hate it when there is a hole in your pocket and your money falls out?

Don't you hate it when your neighbor's dog steals a burger off your barbecue?

Don't you hate it when the second-hand store refuses to refund your underwear purchase?

Don't you hate it when someone steals the prize out of your cereal box?

Don't you hate it when the waiter delivers your meal to another table?

Don't you hate it when you get fired on your day off?

Don't you hate it when your employer declares bankruptcy before you cash your paycheck?

Don't you hate it when you tell the truth and fail a lie detector test?

Don't you hate it when you bust your wife sleeping with your best friend?

Don't hate it when the person in front of you in the buffet line up farts?

Don't you hate it when you realize that you just used an expired condom?

Don't you hate it when your neighbor rats you out to the authorities?

Don't you hate it when your neighbor's dog poops in your vegetable garden?

Don't you hate it when someone sneezes all over the buffet?

Don't you hate it when you are getting a lap dance and the stripper accidentally pees on you?

Don't you hate it when someone twice your size sits in front of you at the movie theater?

Don't you hate it when the person sitting next to you on a twelve hour airplane flight hasn't showered in a decade?

Don't you hate it when people come to your house without notice?

Don't you hate it when the cable goes out during the Super Bowl?

Don't you hate it when you forget to buy a lottery ticket and your lucky numbers are the winning combination?

Don't you hate it when a telemarketer gives you a wake-up call?

Don't you hate it when you recognize your boyfriend on a "Wanted" poster?

Don't you hate it when the elastic on your underwear gives out?

Don't you hate it when your car dies on the way to the hospital emergency unit?

Don't you hate it when you taste a bug as you bite into an apple?

Don't you hate it when you find something valuable and your buddy claims that it belongs to him?

Don't you hate it when you drive two hours to learn that the roads ahead are closed?

Don't you hate it when your employee calls you hon?

Don't you hate it when someone changes the radio station while your favorite song is playing?

Don't you hate it when you are pole dancing and your butt gets bubble gum on it?

DON'T ASK DUMB QUESTIONS!

Don't you hate it when you are a nickel short of getting a soda and the vending machine won't give back your money?

Don't you hate it when your alarm clock malfunctions and you are six hours late for work?

Don't you hate it when the radio falls into the bathtub while you are having a bath?

Don't you hate it when your blind date lies about their gender?

Don't you hate it when your date forgets to flush the toilet and leaves you a surprise?

Don't you hate it when your boss uses your keys to clean his ears?

Don't you hate it when your grandfather accidentally drives through your house?

Don't you hate it when the sandwich artist making your lunch quits before completing your sandwich?

Don't you hate it when your car gets totaled and there is a full tank of gas in it?

Don't you hate it when someone breaks into your car and steals your Christmas gifts?

Don't you hate it when someone has a party at your house and doesn't invite you?

Don't you hate it when someone steals your taxicab?

Don't you hate it when your computer freezes up just before sending a ten page email?

Don't you hate it when the washroom lock malfunctions and half the restaurant walks in?

Don't you hate it when someone borrows your clothes and gets compliments on it?

Don't you hate it when the airport Customs agents make you miss your flight because they were giving you an anal cavity check?

Don't you hate it when your freeloading house guests use up all the hot water?

Don't you hate it when you get stuck on the phone with a high maintenance client that takes up your entire lunch break?

Don't you hate it when people take an hour in the washroom?

Don't you hate it when the wrong pizza get's delivered to you?

Don't you hate it when your luggage ends up on the other side of the planet?

Don't you hate it when your neighbor steals your newspaper?

DON'T ASK DUMB QUESTIONS!

Don't you hate it when someone borrows money off you and dies before paying you back?

Don't you hate it when your air conditioner breaks down during a heat wave?

Don't you hate it when your boss catches you moonlighting at the competitor's workplace?

Don't you hate it when your date pees in your hot tub?

Don't you hate it when your in-laws extend their stay?

Don't you hate it when your boss forgets to take his Prozac?

Don't you hate it when your coworkers help themselves to your lunch bag?

Don't you hate it when someone pees on your toilet seat?

Don't you hate it when you cheat on your taxes and get selected for a random audit?

Don't you hate it when someone squats in your house and eats up all your groceries?

Don't you hate it when you get your trench coat stuck on the bus door and you have no clothes underneath?

Don't you hate it when your eye glasses fog up and you end up rear ending the car in front of you?

Don't you hate it when you accidentally crash your own surprise party?

Don't hate it when the store won't return your earrings because there is blood on it?

Don't you hate it when you call a 1-900 phone sex line and the person you're talking kinky to sounds just like your mother?

Don't you hate it when your car gets repossessed and you forget to take the Christmas Gifts out of the trunk?

Don't you hate it when you are on life-support and someone pulls the plug on you?

Don't you hate it when you get accused of cheating on a survey?

Don't you hate it when get evicted from your apartment for using Canadian coins in the washing machine?

Don't you hate it when you are on the Witness Protection program and bump into your enemy?

Don't you hate it when someone serves you flat pop?

Don't you hate it when you are chatting with a hot girl online and your computer crashes?

Don't you hate it when Customs charges you a tariff on your sex toys?

7 GREASIEST QUESTIONS

Is it vulgar to swear on the bible?

Can a straight person be crooked?

Do blanket shops have undercover security?

Is managing a tennis store a tough racquet?

Are soul mates Korean?

Is American Express a train?

Can you get second-hand smoke at a garage sale?

Do con-artists draw pictures of criminals?

Can a female manhandle someone?

Do gay camp grounds have happy campers?

Can a cop bust a boob doctor?

Does having an affair involve going to an amusement park
without your spouse?

Do gorilla marketers advertise at the zoo?

Can blind people eat seafood?

Does a Twelve Step program teach you how to walk?

Do struggling photographers need to focus?

Do cheap people like to put their two cents in?

How the hell do you catch a twenty two?

Which park does the New York Rangers work for?

Are bankrupt musicians deadbeats?

Is it fair to tell a broken hearted vegetarian that there is plenty of fish in the sea?

Do electricians have great connections?

Since crime doesn't pay then is it a volunteer position?

Can you choke if you swallow your pride?

What kind of sound does a mime make when they have an orgasm?

Are call girls telephone operators?

Does the media complain about being pressed for time?

Do wealthy people eat rich food?

Is it kind of kinky to butter someone up?

Do you have to be a giant in order to flip a house?

DON'T ASK DUMB QUESTIONS!

Do highway robbers steal road signs?

Do mountain climbers complain about price hikes?

Can a Hooker get laid-off?

Is a depressed garbage man down in the dumps?

Are bakery franchise owners cookie-cutters?

Does eating gravel hurt?

Can a claustrophobic person be in the closet?

Do garbage men get trashed at parties?

Do firemen put out cease-fires?

Can teachers get fired if they comprise their principles?

Is it healthy for a diabetic person to have a sweet sixteen birthday party?

Do carpenters like to window shop?

Do stupid weightlifters use dumbbells?

Do gatekeepers hoard fences?

Are female Olympic champions considered trophy wives?

Do drunk carpenters enjoy getting hammered?

Do comedians live on funny farms?

When musicians die do they decompose?

Who scouts a scout?

Is there such thing as a heavy year?

Do crazy people have mental thoughts?

Do serial-daters enjoy breakfast dates?

Can you buy currency at a dollar store?

Is a Made Man a butler for the Mafia?

Do fortune tellers work at banks?

Are burglars house broken?

Is a John a prostitute's washroom?

Is Batman a vampire?

Do garbage men sell junk bonds?

Are nervous cliff divers edgy?

Does the dog pound give doggy bags?

Do ex-con musicians have criminal records?

Is the Big Bang Theory a huge orgy?

DON'T ASK DUMB QUESTIONS!

Are role models fat?

Is water a liquid asset?

Do suspicious countries have red flags?

Do bankrupt nudists enjoy losing their shirts?

Do murderers have shotgun weddings?

Are cantaloupes for couples that refuse to run away and get married?

Would it be senseless to make a raw food cookbook?

Have crazy sculptors lost their marbles?

When a janitor dies do they kick the bucket?

Do mass murders kill people in church?

Aren't flaming people worried about getting burned?

How do you draw a blank?

Aren't people who sit on the fence worried about falling off?

Why does Craig have such a long list?

Is sewage a waste of time?

Why are there childproof bottles for adult dosage drugs?

How many menus should a waiter give to a customer with multiple personalities?

Are TV sets incomplete?

Can a promiscuous vegetarian catch crabs?

Does pop culture center around drinking soft drinks?

Do underwear salesmen deliver brief presentations?

If a drink mixer steals does he end up behind bars?

Do accountants have to watch their figures?

Is a check-mark graffiti in Prague?

Do doctors who can't wait lose their patients?

Is a baseball player a good catch?

Where do people get on and off during a nonstop flight?

Do guys get vasectomies in ballrooms?

Does paying the piper involve clearing a plumbing bill?

Can you buy toadstools in furniture shops?

Are dumb people allowed to use Smart Phones?

Are driving instructors motivated and driven?

Do people who live in poverty have poor health?

How can someone be late if they're dead?

Do electricians take power naps?

Do they serve seeds at pity parties?

Was Woodstock a lumber investment?

Is seaweed an aquatic drug?

Is Batman a baseball player?

Is it self-mutilating to walk on pins and needles?

What kind of dumbass salesman would brag about ripping off a poor Eskimo by selling ice to him?

If you work in a cardboard factory is it hard to think out of the box?

8 DUMB R.V. QUESTIONS

How does it work if you live in an R.V and have house arrest conditions?

If you get busted stealing an R.V. which one of the following criminal charges would you be accountable for?

A) Grand Theft Auto

B) Break and Enter

C) Home Invasion

Where do you address a letter going to an R.V.?

Do R.V.'s come with doorbells? If they did it would be a terrible idea to play Nicky Nicky Nine Door. Because if the owner gets angry he might run you over.

If you live in an R.V. then how do you have a garage sale?

If your R.V. gets damaged are you supposed to call a carpenter or a mechanic?

Does the illegal vehicle open liquor rule apply to R.V.'s.?

Do Girl Guides ever sell cookies to R.V.'s?

If you were to valet an R.V. would the driver be considered a house sitter?

Would it be considered sleazy to rent out a R.V. by the hour?

Are people who live in R.V.'s considered homely?

If you live in an R.V. and then sell it, would the sale be subject to capital gains tax?

Can you claim flood damage if you forget to close the sunroof in your R.V.?

If you live in a R.V. and go on a vacation, then are you really on vacation?

If you were attempting to sell a R.V. Would you list it in the real estate or the vehicle section of the newspaper?

If a hitchhiker fell asleep in a R.V. are they crashing for the night?

If you call an R.V. that just crossed state line, then who pays the long distance charges?

If you live in a R.V. and make cookies then are the cookies R.V. made?

If someone is having a party inside an R.V. and your vehicle hits the R.V., then are you a party crasher?

Rather than hiring a maid to clean your R.V. is it cheaper to go to a car wash?

If you are planning to purchase and live in an R.V. then should you take a car loan or a home mortgage?

Wouldn't you agree that people who live in R.V.'s and drive to work shouldn't complain about the commute?

If a cop busts you speeding in an R.V. is it wise to tell the cop you were in a rush to get home?

Would you agree that it's bad karma to knock people who live in R.V.s? Especially if you live in your car?

Don't you agree it's sort of silly to do a drive by shooting on an R.V.?

If you allow a guy to pick you up in an R.V. on your first date, then aren't you moving sort of fast?

If you live in an R.V. is it cheating if you only have recreational vehicle insurance?

How do you help someone to move if they live in an R.V.?

Is windshield wiper fluid an acceptable house warming gift for someone who lives in an R.V.?

If you live in a R.V. and hear a prowler breaking in, should you call the police or drive to the police station?

If you live in a R.V. and your mechanic needs a week to fix it, then where would you sleep?

If you are having sex in your R.V. and forget to close your curtains, then would you be considered an exhibitionist?

Where does Santa Claus enter in an R.V.?

If you run around an R.V. is it considered a home run?

If you leave your child unattended in an R.V. then are they home alone?

If you catch your buddy inside your R.V. on top of your wife, then is he considered a homewrecker?

If your buddy lives in an R.V. would it be incorrect to call him homeboy?

Do trailer park teachers assign R.V. work?

Are you considered homeless if someone steals your R.V. that you live in?

If you encounter a grease fire in your R.V., then should you call the fire department or drive there?

9 TASTELESS QUESTIONS

How much does it cost to charge somebody?

Does Woodstock trade on the Nasdaq Exchange?

Are Dutch ovens made in the Netherlands?

Are Kaiser Buns made for German Emperors?

Is a nutcracker sexual abuse?

Do dateless people eat Stag Chili for dinner?

Do mathematicians enjoy taking a number?

Do recording artists ever complain about getting hurt from all their hits?

Do astronauts pull their pants down on the moon?

Do people forget to take their vitamins during weekdays?

Do cross-eyed teachers have issues with their pupils?

Does anybody know Bigfoot's exact shoe size?

How can you prove that a proofreader wasn't blind?

What is the difference between break and entering and a door crasher special?

DON'T ASK DUMB QUESTIONS!

Do building inspectors enjoy sightseeing?

Can a person with six cents see dead people?

When pilots die do they reach a higher plane?

Why do people mail E's?

Can you quit eating cold turkey cold turkey?

If a cashier dies on the job does that mean they checked out?

Can you burn yourself from opening up a Hotmail message?

Do ghostwriters write scary stories?

Do hypocrites put a "Keep Off The Grass," sign on their lawn?

If a cop bugs your house, do you have to call an exterminator to remove it?

Do mountain climbers enjoy rock music?

Are garbage men considered trashy?

Do great rulers manage stationary stores?

Is club soda a dance bar?

Do nutjobs work in peanut farms?

Do money launders use fabric softeners?

Do pies come from Bakersfield?

Is a Metrosexual someone that likes to do it on the bus?

Does alienating involve Martians?

Does it hurt to be stonewalled?

Is Lake Erie creepy?

Is Fisher-Price the cost of seafood?

Do pilots put their clothes on aircraft hangars?

Do timeshares involve cheap people sharing watches?

Are you allowed to eat After Eights at seven o'clock?

Was everyone in their late thirties during the middle ages?

Is pea soup made in the washroom?

Is a hot flash someone that streaks in a warm climate?

Are gold miners rich children?

Is a raging alcoholic an angry person that likes to drink?

Do cannibals eat ladyfingers?

Do operators have a lot of hang-ups?

DON'T ASK DUMB QUESTIONS!

Do organ donors give away musical instruments?

Do dump trucks supply toilet paper?

Do rock climbers live on the edge?

Is there a pet name for pet?

Do you have to be playing music in order to break up on a good note?

Can you catch laryngitis from a chat room?

Are squash courts designed for food fights?

Is a mango a term used to get rid of men?

Do horses use satellites when it gets dark?

Can you throw away white trash in black garbage bags?

Do carpenters have house parties?

Did they supply cream and sugar at the Boston Tea Party?

Do drug addicts go to high school?

Are benchwarmers reserved?

Do social workers help people make friends?

Is Shepherd's Pie a sheepherder's dessert?

Do plumbers work on orchards?

Do carpenters go to boarding school?

Do old-fashioned people have a classic attire?

Is a cop-out a revolt against the police?

How do you arrest a house?

Do you have to be a jock to get athletes foot?

Do people with racing hearts have upbeat personalities?

Is Ohio a slang greeting?

Can you avoid losing your job if you have a firewall?

Is a wiretap an electric faucet?

Can you buy extinguishers at a fire sale?

Are obese drug addicts high rollers?

Do judges get their lunch by yelling, "order in the court?"

Do veterinarians enjoy playing snakes and ladders?

Are Germans contagious males?

Is Hangman a suicidal game?

Is jonesing the withdrawal of Archie comic books?

Does picking up the slack involve going to the dry cleaners?

Can you charge someone for assault because they threw rice at you during a wedding?

If a person is attempting to zip their pants, are they working on the fly?

Is goldfish expensive seafood?

Was there electricity during the dark ages?

What's the feminine word for manslaughter?

Is there urine in pea soup?

Was Woodstock a lumber hoarding event?

Does Energizer and Duracell have their headquarters in Battery Park?

Are DJ's itchy because they scratch so many records?

Do vegetarians get paid a large celery?

How come it takes a murderer life to complete a sentence?

Do music pirates have ships?

If you believe that ants don't exist then are you ignorant?

Do sailors complain about peer pressure?

Is a condom a stupid criminal?

Does a friendship come with a life jacket?

Should someone send an exterminator to the flea market?

Can you eat a raw cookbook?

Prior to the invention of drawing boards where would people go back to?

How come famous people's birthdays fall on a holiday?

Is downtime a depressed person's watch?

Is a CEO visually restricted in only seeing two letters of the alphabet?

Why do we have to stop in a drive-thru?

Are Girl Guides supposed to give you directions?

What's worse a stupid question or a dumb answer?

Should you call the fire department if you catch someone burning bridges?

Do liars have false alarms?

Do realtors have garage sales?

Is a miscarriage the name of a single woman?

Can you find pictures of fingers and thumbs in a handbook?

Is a bean bag a vegetarian's purse?

Do drunk advertisers enjoy increasing the buzz?

Can vegans walk on eggshells?

Is a press release when a reporter gets fired?

Do people have babies on Labor Day?

Is a kickboxer a warehouse worker with a bad attitude?

Are college freshmen in a hurry during Rush Week?

Do knock knock jokes poke fun at pregnant women?

Did people catch frostbite during the Cold War?

When actors get married on movies do they have to file for divorce after?

Who wears the pants in your house if you live on a nudist colony?

10 CRAPPY QUESTIONS

Is it pointless to egg a vegan's house?

Do cannibals like sweethearts?

Do alcoholic rock climbers get hangovers?

Is a loan shark a large fish that swims alone?

Do garbage men eat junk food?

Do you have to be a mechanic in order to have a garage sale?

Is a one night stand an incomplete bedroom set?

Are ghost towns scary?

Are fortune cookies expensive?

Do proctologists have problems butting out?

Do flower children have florists for parents?

Are the Cardinal's a Catholic baseball team?

Is it wrong to ask an abusive person to kick the habit?

Do astronauts have a down to earth personality?

DON'T ASK DUMB QUESTIONS!

Are pool men professional billiards players?

Do soap salesmen have bubbly personalities?

Is a bypass a rude way of ending a conversation?

How do you confirm if a word was misspelled in the dictionary?

Is an oxymoron someone who doesn't know how to use pimple cream?

How do you fire a fireman?

Do exterminators enjoy bugging critters?

Are banks worried that their employees might lose interest?

How come some gay people are sad?

Where do they make spring water during the winter?

Are dumb people allowed to drive Smart Cars?

Do pawnshops sell missing chess game pieces?

Is the hall of fame a passage to an eighties show?

Why don't they extend medical schools longer so doctors won't have to open private practices?

Do undergraduate alumni have bachelor parties?

Do salesmen in Alaska make cold calls?

Do swingers have parties at playgrounds?

Can you make a resolution of making resolutions?

Is a crappy violinist unstrung?

When a cleaning lady retires does she throw in the towel?

Why are stands made for sitting?

Do homeboys live sheltered lives?

If you know a guy name Joe who gets C's on his report card, then is he average?

Does it make sense for a detective to plant a bug in an exterminator's house?

Do carpenters get homework?

Is Root Beer made from trees?

Did people have candlelight dinners before electricity was created?

Was Y2K a retired fund?

Are you supposed to have a funeral for deadweight?

Do gravediggers who have fallen behind on their work ever complain about being buried?

DON'T ASK DUMB QUESTIONS!

Can you have a backseat driver in a Smart Car?

Are locksmiths low-keyed?

Why isn't chili cold?

Why do people shut off their car stereos when looking for an address?

Do alcoholic painters enjoy getting plastered?

What kind of shoes do politicians wear when running for office?

Do children come from the Fountain of Youth?

Is Wonder Bread food for thought?

How do you return a gifted person?

Is A.D.D. a syndrome for people that aren't good in math?

Will everybody be wealthy during the golden age?

Can watchdogs tell the time?

Do garbage men listen to trashy music?

Is working at a casino a big gamble?

Does your head need stitches if you are open-minded?

Are bakers breadwinners?

Do crackheads have damaged faces?

Is your mother's sister an insect?

Do horny carpenters enjoy getting nailed?

Do muggers work in cup factories?

Is John Doe a baker whose bakery is in the toilet?

Do lawyers eat their lunch at the food court?

Do security guards wear garter belts?

Do people wear baggy pants in crack houses?

Do cannibals eat head cheese?

Are mechanics sexually active because they're well lubricated?

Is working in a muffler shop exhausting?

Do Smurf's make blueprints?

Have worn out lawyers lost their appeal?

Are shoes alive because they have soles?

How can a rabbit with no feet still be lucky?

Is the letter B above sea level?

DON'T ASK DUMB QUESTIONS!

Do telemarketers complain about the heat from working in boiler rooms?

Can you buy a boat from a wholesaler?

Is a dog pound an animal scale?

Do people eat spicy beans in Chili?

Why do rugby players allow prostitutes to play on their teams?

Do homewreckers demolish people's homes causing divorce?

How come there is no such thing as "gentleman luck"?

Is Old Maid a game for servants?

Do cherry pickers gather fruit?

Why do crocked cops make people walk in straight lines?

Do garbage men have dirty minds?

Can you prove that your pen ran out of invisible ink?

Should someone call an ambulance if they see a party crasher?

Do you need a sink to tap dance?

Do you have to have a gun in order to give it your best shot?

Can a paraplegic be a stand-up comedian?

Do people with foot fetishes eat sockeye?

Is a skinny pyromaniac good at burning calories?

Do cupids make love?

Is having a bad habit a bad habit?

Do cardiologists eat hearty meals?

How come the media never picks on the guilty bystanders?

Do by-curious people wonder how to end a conversation?

Do bossy electricians go on power trips for vacation?

Do tree planters go out on a limb?

How come Superman doesn't have any indecent exposure or public nudity charges for changing in phone booths?

Is a checkmate an insecure spouse?

How do you describe an invisible person?

Is Handy Smurf disable?

Can blind people listen to iTunes?

DON'T ASK DUMB QUESTIONS!

Did Thomas Edison enjoy light dinners?

Do you need a stud detector to find a promiscuous male?

What kind of wacko would kill two birds with one stone?

Do people stop in the red-light district?

Are spiders webmasters?

Do people who like dirty dancing need to take a shower?

Can a woman write a Dear John letter to her husband if his name is Frank?

Is it kind of fruity to ask someone for a date?

Does everybody have big boobs in Silicon Valley?

Is a hot cougar a souped-up Mercury?

Can you soup-up a Campbell's delivery truck?

If your spouse refuses to buy coffee is that grounds for divorce?

Is a senior citizen a Mexican male geriatric?

Is an Adam's apple located in the Garden of Eden?

Do indecisive birds like to sit on the fence?

Is Central Park a parking lot?

Is it a close call when your neighbor phones you?

If you just moved into an igloo, then is unwise to have a house warming party?

Is a friendship your buddy's boat?

Is a baggage handler another name for a psychiatrist?

CONCLUSION

Can a never ending story have a conclusion?

ABOUT THE AUTHOR

Sidney S. Prasad is an author who is on the quest to make the world laugh. His work is focused on entertaining people with his dry humored novels. Sidney S. Prasad personally believes laughter is the best cure for all of life's ups and downs. Some other humorous books written by Sidney S. Prasad include: How To Piss Off A Telemarketer, Corny Names & Stupid Places, My Bipolar Manager, Misfortune Cookies, Plenty Of Freaks: Are You Sold On Online Dating? and Telemarketer's Revenge: The Customer Is Always Wrong, Bitch!